This book belongs to:

Copyright © 2018 by Ed Shankman and Dave O'Neill

All rights reserved

978-1-64194-000-9

Published by Commonwealth Editions, an imprint of Applewood Books, Inc.
P.O. Box 27, Carlisle, Massachusetts 01741

Visit us on the web at www.commonwealtheditions.com
Visit Shankman and O'Neill on the web at www.shankmanoneill.com

Printed in the United States of America

10 9 8 7 6 5 4 3 2 1

A Whimsical Washington Night

The Adventures of a D.C. Duo

by
Ed Shankman

illustrated by
Dave O'Neill

Commonwealth Editions

Carlisle, Massachusetts

Every night in Washington,
When the zoo is closed and school is done,
As sure as the moon will follow the sun,
Two friends meet to have some fun.

With a wink and a smile, they're off on their way,
Feeling ripe for adventure and ready to play.
I should probably mention, in case I forgot,

That one is a panda.

(The other is not.)

This evening, just as things commence,
They bump into some presidents.
A few hellos, and just like that,

They're playing games
With Lincoln's hat.

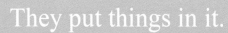

They put things in it.

They cover things up.

They pretend it's a chair

And a face

And a cup.

Will it fly like a Frisbee?

Or spin like a top?

Well, no.
It just plops
To a stop
In the slop.

Soon President George finds a place to relax,
And unpacks a few jacks from the sacks in his slacks.

So they take a few cracks while they're eating their snacks,
But compared to young Daisy, they all look like hacks.

Now they're up for a sword fight so each grabs a twig,
And they jump and they spin in a sword-fighting jig.

But that jumping and jigging stuff ends pretty quick,
Because Roosevelt carries a very big stick!

So they stroll for a while and take in the sights,
Like the fine cherry blossoms (the pinks and the whites)
And the buildings that glow in the bright city lights
Of these dazzling,
Sparkling
Washington nights.

The Supreme Court stands tall with its pillars and all.
And the judges show up with a net and a ball.
Sure, it's nine against five, but our heroes don't care.
'Cause the panda is there and he plays like a bear!

Now they're hiding outside of that cool Spy Museum.
Look deep in the shadows and maybe you'll see 'em.
But is that really them? Can we trust our own eyes?
Is a judge still a judge when he wears a disguise?

Is that President Abe and the panda, or maybe
Just some sweet old lady who's rocking a baby?
And, yes, I confess, it is foggy and hazy,
But that flower pot looks a whole lot like Daisy!

Well, whoever they were, they are gone in a flash,
And they've left their disguises behind in the trash.
They've got places to see. They have much more to do.
They'll keep seeing and doing until they are through!

They are here at the grand Portrait Gallery now,
Where they all paint each other — and let me say, "Wow!"
They work with great care. So much style and grace.
Who knew you could fit so much grace in one face?

Abe captures President Teddy exactly,
While George paints the panda bear much more abstractly.
The panda himself pictures George as an elf,
And I'm telling you, friends, that is one for the shelf.

There are lines.
There are shapes.
There are colors galore.
Go ahead with the red. That's what colors are for.
If you ever want color but aren't quite sure,
Just dip that brush in there and splash on some more!

The judges paint Daisy, then she paints the judges.
They nudge her along so she makes a few smudges.
She covers the smudges with smidges of ridges
And midges with badges and pigeons on bridges.

The others come near and they marvel at how
What they judged to be smudged is a masterpiece now!
It just goes to show you that some poor beginners
Turn bloopers and flubs into wonders and winners.

Our next stop will take us to Capitol Hill,
Where everything seems kind of quiet until
The girl and the bear take their place on the stair,
And start dancing up there with astonishing flair!

They kick to the left and they kick to the right.
They dip and they flip and they rise to full height.
Now the presidents join in; they jitter and jive.
Have you ever seen history come so alive?

They leap and they swivel.
They shimmy and shake.

(But I think I saw Roosevelt make a mistake.)

Now here come the judges — a-swingin' and swayin'.
They grab a few instruments now and they're playin'.
That judge in the corner is really a hit,
And look at Abe Lincoln — he's doing a split.

But wait just one minute —
'Cause there goes our panda.
He's pandering there
On the central veranda!

Just when we wonder what more can be done,
All one hundred senators join in the fun.
They move and they groove. They rock and they roll.
They're dodging and weaving; they're out of control!

We are seeing a marvel, a blast, a sensation,
A bona fide bash in the heart of our nation.
It's pleasure and glee of the highest degree —
An honest-to-goodness D.C. jamboree!

Clearly, there's nothing quite like gettin' crazy
With Washington Panda and his friend D.C. Daisy.

After all the excitement they find a nice place,
Where they lie on their backs gazing up into space.
Then President George turns to President Ted,
And points out the tower that's just overhead.

Daisy feels lucky
To have her friends there —
Presidents, judges,
And one panda bear.

They're a typical gang,
Just like folks everywhere.
(So why are those cars
Pulling over to stare?)

A short while later, the judges depart,
With their net and their ball and a fine work of art.
Then the presidents leave with a heartfelt farewell.
Just where will they go? I don't know. Who can tell?

But it's suddenly clear, as they fade from our view,
That the evening is ending, as all evenings do.
(Though our friends will recall it all, minute by minute,
Reliving each moment long after they're in it.)

It's now time to leave, so that's what they do.
They make their way slowly on up to the zoo.
There's no sweeter delight than a stroll in the night.
Every step feels so perfectly, pleasantly right.

Walking slowly, of course, is much better than fast,
When you want to make sure that a moment will last.
But once they arrive, it is time for good-bye,
So they turn to each other and stand eye to eye.

Then the bright little girl with the long, braided hair
Gives a pat on the head to that big panda bear.

There is no cause for tears. There is no need for sorrow.
Another adventure awaits them tomorrow!

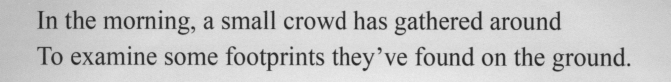

In the morning, a small crowd has gathered around
To examine some footprints they've found on the ground.

Where did those come from? They don't have a clue.
But I know the answer.

And I think you do too.

The End

ALSO by Ed Shankman and Dave O'Neill

Also by Ed Shankman with Dave Frank

Ed Shankman

Ed Shankman's entire life has been one long creative project. He has been writing children's books since he himself was a child. He performed for many years as a lead guitar player and is an impassioned, if imperfect, painter. He has also published his novel, *The Backstage Man*, which was written over the course of three decades. And he has spent his professional career directing creative teams within the advertising industry. Today, Ed lives in New Jersey with his wife, Miriam, who is the love of his life, and their cat.

Dave O'Neill

Dave O'Neill is an Illustrator and Art Director. Throughout his career, Dave has worked with several advertising and marketing agencies where he specialized in children's brands and event planning, but he'd rather be drawing pandas playing volleyball. When he's not drawing pandas playing volleyball, he moonlights with an improv comedy troupe and designs toys in his spare time. This is Dave's tenth book with Ed, and the duo agree that it's time for a movie studio to approach them about an "I Met a Moose" movie. Today, Dave is a husband to a cool girl and a father to a cool, smaller girl. More of Dave's work can be found on his art blog, at oneilldave.blogspot.com.

www.shankmanoneill.com